Guide

STEWARDSHIP

Yes, it's about money, but a whole lot more—using God's resources responsibly

By Herb Mather
For the General Board of Discipleship

STEWARDSHIP

This book is printed on acid-free paper.

ISBN 0-687-03649-6

MANUFACTURED IN THE UNITED STATES OF AMERICA

CONTENTS

Our Identity, Call, and Mission

You are so important to the life of the Christian church! You have consented to be among a great and long line of people who have shared the faith and led others in the work of Jesus Christ. We have the church only because over the millennia people like you have caught the vision of God's kingdom and have claimed a place in the faith community to extend God's love to others. You have been called and have committed your unique passions, gifts, and abilities in a position of leadership, and this guide will help you understand some of the elements of that ministry and how it fits within the mission of your church and of The United Methodist Church.

"The mission of the Church is to make disciples of Jesus Christ. Local churches provide the most significant arena through which disciple-making occurs" (*The Book of Discipline of The United Methodist Church, 2004,* ¶120). The church is not only local but also global, and it is for everyone. Our church has an organizational structure through which we work, but it is a living organism as well. Each person is called to ministry by virtue of his or her baptism, and that ministry takes place in all aspects of daily life, not just within the walls of the church. Our *Book of Discipline* describes our mission to proclaim the gospel and to welcome people into the body of Christ, to lead people to a commitment to God through Jesus Christ, to nurture them in Christian living by various means of grace, and to send them into the world as agents of Jesus Christ (¶121). Thus, through you—and many other Christians—this very relational mission continues. (The *Discipline* explains the ministry of all Christians and the essence of servant ministry and leadership in ¶¶125–137.)

Essential Leadership Functions

Five functions of leadership are essential to strengthen and support the ministry of the church: identifying and supporting leaders as spiritual leaders, discovering current reality, naming shared vision, developing action plans, and monitoring the journey. This Guideline will help you identify these elements and set a course for ministry.

Lead in the Spirit

Each leader is a spiritual leader and has the opportunity to model spiritual maturity and discipline. John Wesley referred to the disciplines that cultivate a relationship with God as the "means of grace" and suggested several means: prayer, Bible study, fasting, public and private worship, Christian conversation, and acts of mercy. Local church leaders are strongly encouraged to identify their own spiritual practices, cultivate new ones as they grow in their own faith, and model and encourage these practices among their ministry team participants.

Discover Current Reality

"The way things are" is your current reality. How you organize, who does what, how bills get paid and plans get made are all building blocks of your current reality. Spend time with people who have been in this ministry and with your committee members to assess their view of how things are. Use "Christian conversation," one of the means of grace, not only to talk to others openly about their understanding of current reality but also to listen for the voice of God regarding your area of ministry.

Name Shared Vision

"The way things are" is only a prelude to "the way you want things to be." When the church is truly of God, it is the way God would envision it to be. Spend time with your committee and with other leaders in the church to discern the best and most faithful future you can imagine. How can you together identify your role and place in a faithful community that extends itself in its fourfold mission of reaching out and receiving people in the name of God, relating people to God, nurturing them in Christ and Christian living, and sending them forth as ministers into the world? Examine your committee's role and its place in that big picture and try to see yourselves as God's agents of grace and love.

Develop Action Plans

How do you get from here (your current reality) to there (your shared vision)? As a leader, one of your tasks is to hold in view both what is and what is hoped for so that you can build bridges to the future. These bridges are the interim goals and the action plans needed to accomplish the goals that will make your vision a reality. Remember that God may open up many (or different) avenues to that future, so be flexible and open to setting new goals and accepting new challenges. Action plans that describe how to meet interim goals should be specific, measurable, and attainable. While it is faithful to allow for the wondrous work of God in setting out bold plans, balance that boldness with realism. You and your committee will find information and tips here on developing and implementing the shared vision, the goals toward that vision, and the specific action plans that will accomplish the goals.

Monitor the Journey

A fifth responsibility of leaders is to keep an eye on how things are going. Setbacks will surely occur, but effective leaders keep moving toward their envisioned future. Not only will you monitor the progress of your committee's action plans to a faithful future but you will also be called to evaluate them in light of the ministry of the rest of the church. Immerse yourself and your plans in God's love and care. Voices from the congregation (both pro and con) may be the nudging of God to shift direction, rethink or plan, or move ahead boldly and without fear. Faithful leaders are attentive to the discernment of the congregation and to the heart of God in fulfilling the mission of the church.

Stewardship: The Call and Its Roots

> *Think of us in this way, as servants of Christ and stewards of God's mysteries. Moreover, it is required of stewards that they be found trustworthy* (1 Corinthians 4:1-2).

What Is a Steward?

Are you confused about *stewardship* and what is expected of you as chairperson of stewardship in your congregation? There is little agreement about what "stewardship" means, so let's trace its roots. "Steward" (from Olde English *stygeward*) referred to the keeper (ward) of the pig sty. The stygeward did not own the pigs but was a responsible farm hand with oversight of the entire hog farming operation. The extended farm family (including all of the hired help) had enough to eat and a decent livelihood if the stygeward did his job well.

"Steward" (translated from the Greek New Testament word *oikonomous,* which shares the root for *economy*), referred to the servant responsible for purchasing supplies, overseeing the other hired hands, keeping the books, and administering the operation of the household. Literally, *oikonomous* means "manager of the household." More than once, Jesus told a story that began, "There was a steward who . . . ."

From both biblical and agrarian images, then, we are all stewards of *God's* household, which first is the whole of creation. Humankind was placed in the midst of God's good creation and told to take care of it (see Genesis 2:15). This is the background and foundation for all stewardship action, whether we administer our own household, the church, the community, the nation, or the world. There are ecological, economic, and geopolitical implications to God's call to be stewards of all that God has created. What we do through our congregations is in the context of the divine reign over all creation, which Jesus described as "the kingdom of God."

Furthermore, the way of life we define as *Christian stewardship* is rooted in the life and teachings of Jesus. When Jesus taught that we should love the Lord our God with all our heart, soul, mind, and strength, he called us to confront seriously the reality of God, who demands justice and abundantly shares compassion, mercy, love, and forgiveness to all. Jesus also called us to love our neighbors as ourselves. Self-acceptance and acceptance of others are interwoven—they cannot be pulled apart without destroying the whole fabric. There is no love of neighbor without love of oneself. Our actions are rooted in God's love for us in Jesus Christ. (See 1 John 4, especially vv. 9-10.) When we know that we are loved, we are free to share that love with others. We cannot give what we have not received.

Stewardship starts with one's relationship to God. The good steward is one whose actions are in alignment with God (the Creator and "owner" of all that the steward manages). Thus, the beginning point for you as the chairperson of stewardship in your congregation is to listen to the will and wishes of God. Through prayer and discernment, seek alignment with God's hopes for your church, the community where your church is located, and for the whole world. Read the Scriptures. Meditate. Listen to what God is saying to you through your reading, through the world around you, through times of worship, and especially through your church's relationship with "the least of these." (See Matthew 25:31-46.)

We Are All Stewards

We are all stewards of God's mysteries—every one of us. We may be effective stewards or not so effective stewards, but nevertheless, we are stewards all the time. It is not an option.

The setting for us to live as stewards is our daily lives in this real world. Stewardship is "in the world." It is our daily human response to what God has done and is doing as well as our response to what we anticipate God will do in this world. The time for being a steward is now. Does this sound like the way the word *stewardship* is used in your congregation?

How does your understanding of yourself as a steward affect your responsibility as the chairperson for stewardship in your local congregation?

The chairperson (and the whole stewardship ministry area, committee, or office) is responsible for helping the whole congregation look to the welfare of the entire household or community. The community includes the congregation, the geographic community of your church, and the wider community of God's world. You have the responsibility and privilege of helping each person within the congregation develop into a more faithful and effective Christian steward in all of those "communities." What a huge job! What an honor!

Focusing Your Attention

While stewardship is, in some way, the task of every officer, leader, and official group within the congregation, the committee on stewardship will need to focus the task to make it clear and manageable. Two such foci are: (1) What stewardship tasks in your setting are not being addressed by other groups? and (2) What are the gifts of the people in your congregation?

It may seem obvious, but you do not need to do what is already being done by some other ministry group in your congregation. Affirm good stewardship wherever you see it but do not duplicate what is already happening. There is plenty to do without trying to duplicate tasks.

In his great commission (Matthew 28:16-20), Jesus called upon his followers to "make disciples of ALL nations" (emphasis added). Our community—as a part of God's people—is an all encompassing circle with one God as Lord of all. However, God has assigned us a special responsibility to the particular community defined by where we live and work and worship. Your task is to work in this context without losing your perspective on the total picture. As you survey the big picture, look for what is being done, what could be done better or more expansively, and what is not being done well enough or at all.

Where do you see God at work in your community? Those who have eyes to see, let them see! (See Mark 8:17-18.)

You can only oversee or manage what there is—not what you wish you had. No one can "steward" what is not there. Pay particular attention to the gifts of the people within your congregation. You will look for the individual and corporate gifts that are within the congregation and seek to set them free to live faithfully in this world. Recognize that many people do not think they are gifted, but each person is gifted. (See 1 Corinthians 12:7.) Select tasks and responsibilities that people within your congregation have the gifts to do.

In summary, as you grow as a Christian steward, you have the task of helping the whole congregation develop gifts and grace for use in this world in whatever sphere of influence the church has corporately and each person has individually. While working on the pieces, never lose sight of the whole.

The Individual as Steward

Stewardship is not an annual financial campaign but a way of life. Individuals become more faithful and effective stewards when they grow into this way of life, involving all that they are, all that they have, and all that they do.

What steps will you make in the stewardship of time?

____

____

What changes do you want to make in the way you use your influence within your family setting, in your church, at work, and in the community?

____

____

What steps will you make in the stewardship of money and possessions? What is God saying to you about the way you save, spend, invest, and give money?

____

____

What is God saying to you about the ways in which you care for the air, the soil, and the water? What ways can you encourage your community to care for the creation?

____

____

These are stewardship questions.

Settings for Exercising Our Stewardship

We are called upon to be stewards within our families. Each of us has responsibility within our homes and in other personal interactions, regardless of our age or other factors.

We are stewards of the gifts, talents, and abilities that God has given us within the church and the community. Review Romans 12, 1 Corinthians 12, and Ephesians 4 to see Paul's lists of gifts that he identified in the churches of his day. Which of these gifts do you see in your own life? Which do you see in the lives of those on your committee or ministry area? Develop the skill for identifying the gifts in others within the congregation. When you have practiced identifying gifts in one another, begin looking for giftedness in the people within your community. Encourage people to use their gifts in their homes, in the community, in the church, and throughout the world.

We are stewards of time. We make decisions about how we spend our time. We either find rhythms in life or we lack rhythm in life. The primary question is how one uses 24 hours of each day; how we (consciously or unconsciously) allot time to prayer and worship, to family and friends, to work, and to recreation. These are stewardship decisions that need to be reevaluated regularly.

None of us can escape being a steward of God's possessions. This includes our handling of money and other resources. Jesus told story after story about one's relationship to possessions. He taught in the tradition of the prophets when he related one's use of possessions to one's relationship with God. In our capitalistic economy, being a Christian steward of our money and possessions may be the most difficult challenge that many of us face.

We model stewardship through our actions and attitudes, by serving and giving. The Christian steward willingly worships, studies, gives, serves, and loves with joy and gratitude as a response to God's grace. Every member, and in particular the members of the stewardship ministry, sets an example by the way we communicate ideas, teach stewardship ideals and identify stewardship opportunities, and exercise our gifts in a variety of ways for the good of the community.

Christian stewardship is not an effort to create a relationship with God, although it may lead to a deepened relationship. It is a response to God because of the joyful relationship that already exists. The response to the invitation to Christian stewardship is part of an on-going, faithful, spiritual journey that deepens and matures.

As members of this congregation, will you faithfully participate in its ministries by your prayers, your presence, your gifts, and your service?

The Church as Steward

> *Do all in your power to increase* their *faith, confirm* their *hope, and perfect* them *in love*. (From the ritual for reception into membership on pages 38 and 43, *The United Methodist Hymnal)*

When persons are received into membership in a United Methodist church, they are asked questions of faith and intention. After the new members respond, the pastor turns to the congregation and asks those assembled to take responsibility for the spiritual growth and nurture of these new members. The congregation is asked to do all in its power to **increase faith**, **confirm hope**, and **perfect** these new members **in love**.

What actions by the congregation will help new members increase faith, confirm hope, and grow in love?

While this commendation is a call upon the church as a body, it can also be the mission statement for the ministry area on stewardship. Stewardship is a year-round assignment for your congregation. Individuals are encouraged, guided, and formed into becoming more faithful Christian stewards through congregations. Congregations who model and develop faithful stewardship encourage their members and constituents to grow spiritually. There is rarely movement unless it starts with the example of clergy and lay leadership who are growing as more faithful and effective Christian stewards.

How does your congregation equip its members to use their gifts and grace for good in the world?

The congregation is a steward in the way it celebrates joys and weeps with those who go through times of sorrow. Sharing is at the heart of stewardship. An act of stewardship may be to develop an email list so that prayer requests can be sent out immediately to all of the people within the congregation.

A congregation is a steward when it organizes a neighborhood clean-up campaign.

The church is a steward when it unlocks its doors during the week and invites the entire community to come in for prayer and meditation.

A congregation is a faithful steward when its business meetings are worthwhile. Groups meet for business when they have something to do—and only then. Disagreements are honored, and all persons struggle for consensus. Caring for one another is a key ingredient of each gathering.

The congregation is a steward in the ways it makes use of its properties. Some congregations seek to *protect* the property more than to *utilize* the property in ministry. A stewarding congregation sees the church building as a resource for the community rather than a clubhouse for its members.

The congregation is a steward in the manner in which the money is received and handled. [See *Guidelines for Leading Your Church: Finance* for more details.] Every giver expects that the funds are being handled properly. This is not a new issue. Read 2 Corinthians 8:16-23 to see the lengths to which Paul went to assure the Corinthians that their offerings would get to where they were intended.

The congregation is a steward of the funds that are given for mission and ministry. Churches need to be open and candid about where funds are spent—which ministry is fulfilled because of this giving. Every person's concern must be taken seriously. However, that does not mean that every person will agree with every decision.

The church is a good steward when it manages the funds well—keeping good records and making responsible decisions about allocations of funds. The financial life of the church needs to be "transparent" so that all have access to the way the financial life of the congregation is conducted.

How Does Stewardship Ministry Fit into the Congregation's Organizational System?

The chairperson of the ministry area on stewardship is elected annually by the charge conference after being nominated by the committee on lay leadership or from the floor of the charge conference. This chairperson is a member of the finance committee. In some congregations, stewardship is the responsibility of a sub-committee of the committee on finance. Smaller congregations often find that this is their best (or only) alternative. The risk in making stewardship a part of the finance committee is that stewardship may be thought of only in terms of money or that day-to-day management issues will overshadow the other theological implications of a life of stewardship. When a distinct group has the sole responsibility for planning and encouraging year-round growth in faithful stewardship, the whole congregation is likely to benefit.

Each United Methodist congregation has the freedom and responsibility to organize itself, within the boundaries defined by the *Book of Discipline*, so your church may be organized a bit differently from others.

Christian spiritual formation is the foundation for dynamic and effective stewardship, regardless of the organizational configuration. The job of the chairperson and the members of the ministry area on stewardship is to inspire and to lead the congregation as growing stewards.

Cooperate with the church council, the pastor(s), and other church leaders to address the needs and opportunities of this ministry area, utilizing all appropriate resources and relationships within your community, the congregation, the district, the annual conference, and the denomination.

What Are My Main Responsibilities as Stewardship Chairperson?

Vigorously resist the perception that the sole task of the ministry area of stewardship is to conduct an annual giving campaign. There is nothing wrong with having an annual giving campaign or in directing one. In fact, an annual giving campaign may be one of your responsibilities, but stewardship is far more than an annual campaign. It is a year-round task, and while it includes money, Christian stewardship includes far more than money.

Your main responsibilities **may** include the following:

(Refer to the Resources at the end of this handbook to help you in these tasks.)

1. **Plan and promote a comprehensive year-round agenda for developing Christian stewards.** This may include stewardship education, giftedness, ecological stewardship, proportionate giving and tithing, guiding an annual giving campaign, planned giving, personal financial management, and developing a Christian lifestyle.

2. **Interpret the biblical and theological basis for Christian stewardship** using resources consistent with the doctrines and polity of The United Methodist Church. An excellent foundational resource is *Steward,* a twelve-session study available from Cokesbury. (See the Resources at the back of this Guideline.)

3. **Promote spending, saving, investing, and giving consistent with a Christian lifestyle.** In a capitalistic culture, this may be one of the greatest challenges facing North American Christians today. Build systems that help people in your church and community escape the strangulating demon of debt.

4. **Invite persons in your congregation to explore tithing** (giving 10 percent) and encourage them to set the tithe as the minimum goal for their giving.

5. **Create, within the congregation, a deepening commitment to personal and corporate Christian stewardship,** which includes taking care of the creation as well as using and sharing talents and resources.

6. **Work with the committee on finance in your church.** Encourage them to review their processes so that the financial aspects of the church are growing more consistent with faithful stewardship theology and practice. Encourage processes that build accountability and trust.

Ask each member of your stewardship group to "vote" on two of the items as their top priorities. Collect the votes and put a check by the ones for which they voted. You will then see the primary concerns of your committee. This will help you to narrow the broad scope of work to where the emphasis can be for this year (or the next three years).

How Should I Start?

1. **If you do not already have a committee, ask the committee on lay leadership to help you** to select a group of persons with the interest and commitment to work with you. Strive to have a group that reflects all the ages within your congregation, including youth.

2. **Ask to meet with the pastor and your committee** to explore your aspirations, dreams, and goals and to align them with the mission and vision of the congregation. Establish clarity about expectations so that you work together and keep the lines of communication open throughout the year.

3. **At the first meeting of your ministry area, pray and reflect together** on where each of you is on your own spiritual journey as a Christian steward. Ask: Where is God calling us to change and grow? Encourage your committee members to take a personal step with you in the direction(s) where God is calling you. A *Money Autobiography* can help you assess your own stewardship (see www.gbod.org/stewardship).

Then spend most of your time listening to the hopes, ideas, and passions of your committee members. List—and celebrate—what the congregation is already doing to foster faithful stewardship. List new ventures for stewardship growth and improvement. The new ventures will probably not emerge clearly at first. When they do, be sure that you enter into them with the passion and planning necessary to follow through on them.

4. **Begin each meeting with prayer or other Christian practice,** thanking God for all blessings and seeking divine guidance for your work. As you assign tasks and check on progress, remember to help each other and to celebrate all of the places where you sense God working in your community and your congregation. Focus on your successes. Learn from failures. Give hope and encouragement to your colleagues on the stewardship team.

5. **Simplify your meeting agenda** so that, instead of referring to old business and new business, you include three items: informational items, study items for discussion only, and action items (previous study items on which you now take action). Seek consensus where possible without voting and always aim for a positive conclusion to discussions. Allow time for members to share their own personal struggles and growth as Christian stewards.

6. **Decide how often to meet** (monthly, bi-monthly, quarterly). Meet often enough to maintain continuity between meetings and long enough to accomplish a reasonable agenda.

7. Plan the tasks you need to accomplish during the year, such as year-round stewardship education, an annual giving campaign, or other projects. Link the people with those themes and issues that excite them. Set them free to do their work. Do not micro-manage, but regularly encourage them.

8. Keep each meeting of your group focused on who you are as Christian stewards more than on what activities you can think up for the church. Pause for times of meditation, prayer, or singing in the midst of your meetings. As a response, use "All Things Come of Thee" (588, *The United Methodist Hymnal*) or another of your choosing.

Forming Stewards Within the Congregation

Consider the following action items for adaptation and use in your congregation. SELECT ONLY THOSE ACTIONS that will enhance the primary task you wish to accomplish this year. Convey both information and inspiration. Communicate through a variety of ways in order to reach many individuals. Redundancy in method is essential!

Values and Goals

All activity is in the context of a set of values and accepted goals. Each one of the items listed below has implied values and may be considered a goal to be achieved. This list is directed more towards financial stewardship.

1. Focus on the need of the giver to give rather than on the need of the church to receive. Focus on God's love and one's response to it in the totality of life. Giving through the church of one's time emphasizes living one's life as a Christian twenty-four hours each day, seven days a week.

2. Change is more likely to come through modeling and invitation than through argument. When peoplen model faithful stewardship others are encouraged to live their faith in this secular world. Recognize that it is not easy. Fortify one another.

3. Encourage your church leaders and other members to envision the future. Listen to the dreams and hopes regardless of a person's age, spiritual maturity, or office in the church. Listen especially for persons to say, "Why don't we . . . ?"

4. Work toward the goal in the next five to ten years of giving 20 percent or more of the church's total annual offerings, including special offerings and outreach gifts, toward local and denominational benevolences. This goal could be achieved by giving 10 percent or more of the church's total annual offerings to local community needs and 10 percent or more to denominational and worldwide missions in addition to apportionments for annual conference and denominational ministries. This enables those whose passion is local needs and those who care most about worldwide missions to each feel that they are involved in giving toward these causes.

Communication

It is essential to keep lines of communication open among all members of the congregation, especially between laity and clergy. When clergy are informed of giving levels, especially of any sudden changes in the pattern of a family's giving, they can follow up and see if there is a joy to celebrate or pain to work through. An increase, for example, may mean a big bonus, or a decrease may be due to serious illness or separation or divorce or job loss. With such knowledge the clergy are better able to relate to the real life of the laity in the congregation.

It is also important to keep lines of communication open between all age levels in a congregation. Children and youth in their Sunday school classes and other groups can discover the joy of giving. Children are usually eager to have their own offering envelopes. They love to hear the stories of the good that is done with the money they give. Affirm the small acts of sharing that children do for one another and for their parents and other adults.

1. **Include articles on stewardship monthly in the church newsletter.**

2. **Plan a "Stewardship Moment" once a month during the worship service** with different individuals speaking for one minute on a stewardship theme, such as the stewardship of personal influence or the stewardship of personal relationships, the joy in giving, or their spiritual journey with tithing (or toward tithing). If someone visited a ministry supported through missions, invite that person to tell the others a human-interest story about the ministry.

3. **Invite the children in Sunday school to prepare posters** illustrating the concept(s) of living with God's creation and their understanding of sharing time, talent, and treasure. Children have high ideals about sharing. Display the posters prominently, remembering to announce the display and to list, with thanks, all of the children's names in the weekly bulletin.

One congregation asked the children to make posters describing sharing. These posters were "posted" on a wall of the church on the Sunday designated for "One Great Hour of Sharing." Persons in the congregation were urged to bid on a poster by attaching a check or cash to the "ballot" that was put in a basket. The highest bid would get the poster, but all the funds went to the One Great Hour of Sharing offering.

4. Create special offering envelopes for children. In addition to the envelop as a place for them to insert their offering money, provide a place on the outside for the children to tell of ways they have given of their time or shared something else during the week. Once each month, print these (edited) statements in your church newsletter.

5. Schedule a discussion session with the youth about setting priorities for the use of time and money. Ask them to prepare banners illustrating the passions and ideas around a stewardship theme. Display the banners prominently, remembering to announce the display and to list, with thanks, all of the youths' names in the weekly bulletin.

6. Display pictures, cartoons, short quotes, and articles on stewardship on the church bulletin board. Change the display often. Place current pamphlets and leaflets on stewardship published by our denomination in literature racks. Keep them current.

7. Work with the ministry team on worship to include the names of ministries being funded through the church's stewardship in morning prayers.

8. Invite those who enjoy acting to perform a chancel drama on stewardship. The script could either be written by a local church member or obtained from denominational resources.

Education and Inspiration

1. Encourage clergy to preach on stewardship throughout the year and to call persons to be faithful stewards.

2. Arrange a forty-five-minute session with the ministry team on worship. Explore ways to make the time of the offering in worship a great time of joy and celebration.

3. Use stewardship study resources for small groups, like *Steward: Living as Disciples in Everyday Life*. (See Resources and check with your Conference Media Library for the availability of these resources.)

4. Plan one-day or weekend retreats focusing on how to become good stewards, using denominational publications and other resources available.

5. Offer a series of study sessions on the biblical concept of tithing. Use for your text *Holy Smoke! Whatever Happened to Tithing?* by J. Clif Christopher and Herb Mather.

6. Conduct workshops throughout the year on the following related topics: (1) Christian Money Management; (2) Estate Planning; (3) Wills; (4) Deferred Giving; (5) Trusts and Bequests. Secure leadership from your annual conference's stewardship foundation or a similar organization. Invite members of neighboring churches. This gives opportunity for discussion and fellowship in a larger group than just your own church and is good stewardship of the leader's time.

Year-Round Stewardship

What would "year-round" stewardship look like? The materials that follow are a guide—not a blueprint. This section begins with an approach to the task and then moves to possible ingredients for consideration at appropriate times throughout the year. You will need to adapt the suggestions and recommendations to your particular situation. You will find alternate scenarios. Select only those components that are appropriate for your congregation.

Recommended Components for a Twelve-Month Plan

Subject Matter

1. Stewardship of the Creation. Contact the General Board of Church and Society (www.umc-gbcs.org or call 1-202/488-5650) for resources and suggestions in this area.

2. Personal Financial Management. This may be the most needed area for many individuals and families in your congregation. Many people are controlled by the demon of debt rather than living in the fullness of financial freedom. Help people take control of their finances with the guidance of faith and the support of the fellowship. (See "The Stewardship of Money and One's Personal Finances," page 27.)

3. Tithing. The tithe is a helpful God-given benchmark for giving. See Resources for recommendations.

4. Time, Talent, and Giftedness. People are the church even when they are not doing "church work." Expand your horizons to find ways to help people use their gifts beyond working on a church committee. Affirm the variety of ways people use their gifts and talents seven days a week. (See "Spiritual Gifts," pages 26-27.)

5. Planned Giving and Estate Planning. (See page 23.)

Actions & Programs

6. Celebration. Look for reasons to celebrate the good things done through the ministry and outreach of your congregation. Help the people feel good about the difference they are making in the world through their prayers, presence, gifts, and service.

7. Personal Witness. Never underestimate the power of personal testimony. Invite generous persons to share about the struggles and joys of their giving pilgrimage.

8. Preaching. The Bible contains a wealth of preaching material on a variety of stewardship issues. (See www.gbod.org/stewardship for sermon starters.)

9. Telling the Stories. Find ways to tell stories of the difference made in the lives of people through their giving through this congregation. This may be done at the time of the offering or at another place in the worship service. Select stories and pictures for your newsletter. Send brief stories via email to your members and constituents. For specific stories about the apportioned funds and special offerings, go to the Web site www.umcgiving.org and find stories about apportioned funds, the Advance, special Sundays, special appeals, and conference benevolences.

10. Intentional Study Sessions on Stewardship Issues. Short-term studies are available on a variety of Christian stewardship issues. Consider speakers and programs at special events in your church. (See *Steward* and *Wesley and Giving* in Resources.)

11. An Annual Emphasis. At least once each year, intentionally call upon the people to evaluate their giving in the light of their spiritual growth. This may be done through an annual giving campaign.

The eleven components above are divided into two groupings. The first group (1-5) is subject matter. The second group (6-11) includes actions and programs. Actions and programs communicate subject matters. Then you will move to possible settings where the actions and programs can communicate the subject matter.

Settings

Examine each of the above eleven components and explore the settings where each is most appropriate within your congregation or parish. Settings will vary depending upon the size and "style" of the congregation. Settings may include (but are not limited to):

- worship services
- children's classes and groups
- youth classes and groups
- adult classes and groups
- confirmation classes
- adult new member orientation/formation groups
- United Methodist Women and United Methodist Men
- programs at Fellowship Dinners and Family Night Programs
- traditional annual celebration events.

Scenario 1: A Year-Round Model

The following scenario is arranged with possibilities for actions taken weekly, monthly, quarterly, semi-annually, and annually.

Weekly

- Pray (daily).
- The offering in worship can be a time of helping persons effectively and creatively see the relationship between giving and faith. Meet with the worship ministry area to explore ways the offering can express our professing faith.
- How is the offering received in children's Sunday school classes? Meet with the education ministry area to explore ways to communicate the joy of giving to the children and youth and to help them celebrate that they are part of spreading the good news of Jesus Christ throughout the community and around the world.

Monthly

- Invite a generous giver to offer a testimony about giving during the worship service. (Generosity is not determined by amount but by proportion.)
- Send letters written by members of the church to all persons on your membership and constituency lists. Writers can express what the church means to them or something of their own pilgrimage in giving. (Order Letters For All Seasons on a floppy disc—Microsoft Word format—for $7 from h.mather@comcast.net.)
- Creatively say "Thank You" (over and over again) to the people of the congregation for their giving.
- Use the church bulletin boards to communicate human-interest stories about the difference their giving is making in the lives of people all over the world.

- Mail offering envelopes for each month instead of distributing annual boxes.
- Place a brief article in your church newsletter urging participation in the church endowment fund.

Quarterly

- Hold a new member formation class that includes a session on responsible personal finance and giving.
- Send a letter to every giver, thanking each for his or her gift and recording the total amount received to date from him or her. (This can be one of the monthly letters noted above and may include the monthly giving envelopes.)
- Bring a group together to write a brief humorous skit about giving. Present the skit at a church dinner or in a worship service.
- Schedule a brief "stewardship education" segment at the meeting of the church council.

Semi-Annually

- Hold a ministry and mission fair. A fair is a good time for various groups (from prayer groups to work groups to fun groups) to seek to enlist others into their group or task. It is a time of celebration.
- Publish a step chart listing the numbers—not names—of persons/families giving at each giving level above $10 per week.

Annually

- Offer short-term studies on stewardship using materials such as *Steward*.
- Hold an annual emphasis on giving. You may use a self-directed campaign to guide the leadership in helping persons relate their giving to their spiritual pilgrimage. A list of companies who sell self-directed campaign programs is available at: www.gbod.org/stewardship.

Scenario 2: A Four-Part (Quarterly) Model

Develop a quarterly design to guide your work in stewardship. This design is shaped around four specific areas listed in the questions asked of each new member: prayers, presence, gifts, and service. It is especially appropriate in smaller membership congregations where all activity is led by a committee-of-the-whole. These four emphases may be rearranged in order to fit the needs of your congregation. Your ministry area may be responsible for only one or two parts of the whole design with other groups in the church leading the other components.

Prayers. During one quarter of the year, emphasize the stewardship of one's prayer life. Develop short-term classes on prayer. Urge each Sunday School class, youth group, women's circle, and men's group to have at least one prayer emphasis during this quarter. You can broaden the scope of this emphasis to include the "means of grace" described by John Wesley, which included Bible study, both family and personal prayer, the Lord's Supper, and fasting or abstinence. Work with your nurture ministry area or committee to develop this emphasis.

Presence. During one quarter of the year, develop a specific plan for encouraging persons to attend worship regularly. This may include regular telephone calls to persons, and providing additional opportunities for worship. Provide models of brief worship times that can be used by committees, organizations, and groups within the church when they meet so that there is more than a perfunctory prayer to open a meeting. Work with the worship ministry area or committee to develop plans for this emphasis.

Gifts. Celebrate the good that is being done through the financial giving of persons within your congregation. During this quarter, find some legitimate way to celebrate giving every week. Help persons take charge of their own financial life rather than being slaves to debt. Provide financial planning workshops. Work with the committee on finance to develop a plan for inviting persons to evaluate whether their financial giving is keeping up with their spiritual growth. A giving campaign may be appropriately used during this emphasis.

Service. The service emphasis will emphasize the spiritual gifts as described in 1 Corinthians 12, Romans 12, and Ephesians 4. Develop a plan to encourage members to identify their spiritual gifts and to use them in the church and in the world. Relate the gifts and passions of the people to the needs of the community and the world. Celebrate the many ways people are already using their gifts for the joy of serving and the glory of God. A talent fair can be an appropriate and helpful activity for this emphasis.

Scenario 3: Another Four-Quarter Model

If your responsibility is to emphasize four different kinds of financial stewardship during the year, the following model may be adapted and used in your congregation. Work closely with the committee on finance as you develop this year-round strategy.

First Quarter: Personal Finance. Plan a series of special sessions on personal finance for each generational group within your congregation. For instance, you may have a series of sessions for parents of young children on "How to have enough money so your children can go to college." For middle adults the session(s) could be on "Money and your teenager" or "How to retire without living in the poor house." For older adults the sessions may be on estate planning or on planned giving options, "Living long without outliving your money." You could even have an "altar call" in a worship service when you invite members to come to the altar of the church and cut up their credit cards (provide strong scissors).

Second Quarter: Planned Giving. Using a series of mailings and brief testimonials, describe the many ways to give in addition to cash or check. Potential givers in your congregation may find planned giving tools helpful in their particular situations. For instance, members can give stock, property, insurance policies, and a host of other valuables. If you do not already have an endowment or trust fund committee, invite your conference foundation executive to come to your church and guide you as one is established. Do this even if you have no idea if the church will ever receive any bequest or other endowment gift.

Third Quarter: The Financial Stewardship of the Congregation. Review the budget building process in your church, the financial accountability system you have in place, and the methods you use to communicate financial information to the members and constituents. Hold focus groups of church members to seek ideas for improvement. Work closely with the committee on finance on this project.

Fourth Quarter: Giving. During this quarter, you will ask members to evaluate their giving and to make individual and family commitments for the giving that support the ministries of the congregation. You may work on this emphasis through an annual giving campaign.

Scenario 4: A Modest Start

First Year

If your congregation has no history of intentional activity around Christian stewardship (except for an annual giving campaign) then choose two of the following options as the starting point for your work.

1. Work with those in your congregation who are responsible for shaping the worship service to transform the offering into a time of celebration through testimonies, stories of lives changed through your church's giving. Be willing to experiment with movement and with fresh patterns of action.

2. Develop a narrative budget (the budget as story) to describe the life and ministry of your congregation in human-interest form.

3. Set a time to show the video *Wesley and Giving* to your leaders. Invite others to come as well. Provide an opportunity to discuss the issues raised in the video.

4. Ask your pastor to preach a three-sermon series on the relationship of possessions to one's spiritual life. (Visit www.gbod.org/stewardship for sermon starters.)

5. Show the video "It All Began With a Servant" as part of your Sunday worship (available from United Methodist Communications).

Second Year

Select one of the following items to add to what you launched in the first year.

1. Develop a twelve-month calendar of stewardship that may include but is not limited to one or more of the following:
   - a study of the theology of stewardship
   - giftedness
   - personal and family financial planning
   - estate planning
   - stewardship of the Creation.

2. Add two of the options from the list above to what you are doing.

3. Draw together a group to study *Steward*.

4. Invite a group of key leaders (not necessarily officers) who will make a commitment to the thirty-day process described in *Holy Smoke! Whatever Happened to Tithing?* (See Resources.)

Third and Fourth Years

Look over the items for the two previous years. Evaluate what should be continued and what should be dropped. You may see ways to improve upon what you have done. Then look at the suggestions that you had chosen not to do in those years. It may be that it is now time to add one of those items to the list of what your ministry team will guide to fulfillment during the next year(s).

Generations and Christian Stewardship

Reaching young people is especially important in stewardship, for they are both our current and next generation of stewards. Attractive worship centers and meaningful liturgy can reinforce growth as Christian stewards.

Include the children and youth of the congregation during any stewardship emphasis. Do not shy away from dealing with money issues from a faith perspective. Many youth have a distorted view of money. They have a poor concept of giving through their church. Even very young children can understand the meaning of giving, receiving, and sharing.

Ways to Nurture Young Children as Stewards

- Tell a good story, with action and excitement.
- Use object lessons.
- Describe heroes (biblical and contemporary) worthy of our admiration.
- Teach children to share with others. Affirm them when they do share.
- Teach children to express thanks in their conversations and in their prayers.
- Work with parents of young children to help them communicate healthy faith-based money values to their children. See the "nuggets" on parents, money, and children at http://www.gbod.org/stewardship/articles/.

Ways to Nurture the Youth as Stewards

- Share stories of famous people whose lives were devoted to helping others, such as Albert Schweitzer and Mother Teresa. Invite a generous person from the congregation to share his or her personal testimony of sharing time and money.
- Discover how youth are already volunteering their time in helping others, such as assisting in the church nursery, participating in community service projects, and caring for the environment. Explore additional options with them.
- In Sunday school or other Christian education settings, discuss Scripture references to stewardship and the qualities of a Christian steward.
- In confirmation classes describe the ways stewardship is understood in the Bible including Creation, giftedness, first fruits giving, tithing, and jubilee.
- In youth fellowship meetings provide sessions on budgeting allowance money and money earned from paid employment. Explore the moral and ethical issues around advertising, spending, saving, and investing.
- Include youth in your church's next Volunteers in Mission (VIM) team.

Ways to Nurture Adults as Stewards

- Offer short-term classes on a wide variety of stewardship issues.
- Affirm faithful Christian stewardship when you see it from individuals and from groups.
- Include stewardship in new member formation sessions.
- Model gracious receiving as well as generous giving.

Spiritual Gifts

God has blessed each of us with unique and important gifts. Enabling church members to discover, develop, and use their gifts is another important function of the ministry area on stewardship. Here are some methods by which this may be accomplished.

Plan a Gifts Discovery Workshop. If possible, secure leadership through the annual conference connectional ministries office. In preparation for the above activities, your ministry area can study the following Scriptures: Romans 12:4-8; 1 Corinthians 12:4-31; Galatians 5:22-23; and Ephesians 4:7-13.

Study Spiritual Giftedness. Examine pertinent Scriptures in an elective Sunday School course or in a series of weeknight sessions. Also study and use these important recent books on spiritual gifts: *Equipped for Every Good Work* by Dan R. Dick and Barbara Miller, *Learning to Lead from Your Spiritual Center* and *Spirit Gifts: One Spirit, Many Gifts* by Patricia D. Brown, and *Rediscovering Our Spiritual Gifts* and *Your Spiritual Gifts Inventory* by Charles V. Bryant. (See the Resources.)

Help to orient the mindset of work areas and committees to being inviters of gifts. Instead of using a control model that "runs every idea through a committee" that can veto or radically alter the concept, have the committee see itself as a group that helps gifted persons fulfill God's calling through the life of the congregation. When someone says, "Why don't we . . . ?" ask that person to find three or four other persons who are also interested and help them accomplish their dream.

Plan a ministry fair every six months. Invite anyone who has a legitimate idea for a ministry to set up a display. If that person can find at least four other persons in the church who are willing to "sign on," the idea becomes an official program of the church for the next six months. At the six month anniversary, evaluate, then persons have the opportunity to sign up again for another six months or to move on to try out something else.

> Just as the body without the spirit is dead, so faith without works is also dead (James 2:26).

The advantage of this six-month plan is that many people are afraid to participate in an activity for fear that it will become a long-term commitment. Also, the concept encourages people to dream dreams and to see visions of what the church can become through the commitment of the gifts and grace God has given.

As members explore their gifts and talents and learn to encourage others to share their gifts, the church can better fulfill the ministry of Jesus Christ. Remember that gifts are not for use only within the church. As Christians we are called to be in ministry throughout the world and with *all* of our neighbors, regardless of who they are or where they live. The needs are great. We must respond. Affirm church members as they witness to Christ throughout the local community and the world through active discipleship and service.

The Stewardship of Money and One's Personal Finances

Give opportunity to all church members to give the best of their time, talents, and resources. Encourage them to be good stewards in all facets of their life. The ministry of money and the management of one's personal finances are connected in the lives of all who practice Christian stewardship.

> Where your treasure is, there your heart will be also (Matthew 6:21).

How people handle their personal finances and how they use their money are concerns in modern society. More than two hundred years ago these issues were also concerns of John Wesley, the father of Methodism. He was concerned about the poor and preached to them "where they were." Wesley was also concerned about those followers who did have money, how they acquired it, what they did with it, and the effect of their buying and selling on the whole of society. Wesley, in his sermon "The Good Steward," declared that God has entrusted us with our souls, our bodies, our goods, and whatever other talents we have received.

The church today can provide its people with a valuable service in two particular areas of financial stewardship. First, the stewardship guidance given to persons within the church enables them to establish a healthy relationship with money and material possessions in their own lives. Help in personal financial stewardship encourages individuals to become faithful stewards of their money and their material wealth and to grow to their full potential as Christians. Secondly, the generous giver of financial resources within the church makes possible a strong ministry of outreach to the community.

Nurturing Generosity Through the Church

In most churches, the committee on finance is skilled in managing the funds but may lack the gifts for inspiring generosity. The stewardship ministry group has the freedom to emphasize generosity instead of the management of the church funds. Invite persons to share publicly the joy they have found in generous giving.

There are many ways to give, and some congregations provide many options for giving. In cooperation with the committee on finance, consider some of the following emphases and ventures.

Regular and Proportionate Giving

- Encourage church members to study the Scriptures and learn what Jesus teaches about giving and sharing one's resources as part of one's spiritual growth. (See the article, "Qualities of the Christian Steward" on www.gbod.org/stewardship.)
- Ask church members to determine the percentage of income they now give and to develop a covenant to increase that percentage by 1 percent per year. Be up front that such a decision will cause most persons/families to rearrange priorities in their spending habits.
- Provide opportunities for church members to respond regularly to fund the various ministries of the church locally, nationally, and globally, through envelopes and special offerings for specific needs. Make these moments invitational rather than coercive.
- Offer the option for persons to support the ongoing ministries of the church through monthly automatic debiting of their bank account. For further information go to http://www.gcfa.org/ElectronicGivingInfo.html.

Encourage Tithing as a Spiritual Discipline

- Engage leaders in a small group study such as *Holy Smoke! Whatever Happened to Tithing*? (See the Resources.)
- Ask a person who tithes to share the story of his or her spiritual journey that brought them to the decision to tithe.
- Encourage groups within the church to tithe the funds that they manage. The decision making process about how to spend the tithe helps them explore their values and priorities.

Special Funds

- Whenever there is a special offering, tell the story of its purpose and the hopes for the use of the funds. Then invite those who wish to support that kind of mission to give generously with the knowledge that all of their gift will go to that specific ministry.
- Establish a memorial and honor gift program that provides a channel for giving to the church in memory of or in honor of loved ones. Clearly state the way the funds will be disbursed and provide a "wish-book" of items that families of the deceased or of the honoree may select for the distribution of the monies.
- Establish an endowment fund with well-defined purposes so that church members have the opportunity to fund ongoing ministries through bequests and gifts.
- Provide information on gift annuities, the giving of insurance policies, and the giving of real estate. These provide another avenue of giving and an additional way in which persons may help their church meet its financial obligations and further its ministries.

Financial (or Giving) Campaigns

Many congregations find that it is helpful to create a special task group to lead the giving campaign rather than expecting a standing committee to have the proper personnel and gifts to provide the leadership required. An effective giving campaign needs persons who have imagination—who think outside the box—as well as people who can manage details. Some persons are willing to take on a specific, limited-duration task who are not willing to serve on a committee that meets regularly.

The most effective campaigns for the past two decades have emphasized the spiritual need of the giver to give rather than the need of the church to receive money to meet its budget. Encourage the committee on finance to wait until after the campaign to prepare the budget. If they wish to get started before your campaign, do not publicize the budget as the reason for people to give. The budget is an important document for guiding responsible management of the funds. It does not inspire generosity!

Congregations throughout the nation use various methods to conduct financial campaigns and to enlist the financial commitment of their members. For the latest list of companies and the campaigns they sell, go to the Center for Christian Stewardship web site (www.gbod.org/stewardship). You will find links to a wide variety of campaigns.

Do not use the same campaign more than two years in a row. Each campaign style and language will be received more helpfully by some members of the congregation than by others. If you keep using the same campaign, you will continue to communicate effectively with the same group while missing others.

A campaign is a method of reaping a harvest. The harvest is much more likely to be abundant if you have had an effective year-round process for communicating and celebrating the mission and ministry of the church.

Resources

Center for Christian Stewardship
General Board of Discipleship
P.O. Box 340003
Nashville, TN 37203
877-899-2780 Ext. 7077 www.gbod.org/stewardship

Ecumenical Stewardship Center
1100 West 42nd Street, Suite 225
Indianapolis, IN 46208
www.stewardshipresources.org

Ministry of Money
11315 Neelsville Church Road
Germantown, MD 20876
www.ministryofmoney.org

Theology and Biblical Roots

- *The Dancing Steward,* by Christopher Levan (Toronto: The United Church Publishing House, 1993. ISBN 1-55134-004-6).
- *Full Disclosure: What the Bible Says About Financial Giving,* by Herb Miller (Nashville: Discipleship Resources, 2003. ISBN 0-88177-411-1).
- *God, the Economist,* by Douglas Meeks (Minneapolis: Fortress Press, 1989. ISBN 0-80062-329-0).
- *Learning to Lead From Your Spiritual Center,* by Patricia D. Brown (Nashville: Abingdon Press, 1996. ISBN 0-687-00612-0).
- *Steward: Living as Disciples in Everyday Life,* by Charles Foster (Nashville: Abingdon Press, 1996. ISBN 0-687-09944-7).
- *Wesley and Giving.* Ecufilm video (Nashville: United Methodist Communications, 1999). Call 800-251-4091.
- *Why We Apportion.* A brief theological basis for giving through the United Methodist apportionment system. Download from www.gcfa.org/WhyWeApportion.

Giftedness

- *Equipped for Every Good Work,* by Dan R. Dick and Barbara Miller Dick (Nashville: Discipleship Resources, 2001. ISBN 0-88177-352-2).
- *Rediscovering Our Spiritual Gifts,* by Charles V. Bryant (Nashville: Upper Room Books, 1991. ISBN 0-8358-0633-2).
- *Spirit Gifts: One Spirit, Many Gifts,* by Patricia D. Brown (Nashville: Abingdon Press, 1996. ISBN 0-687-00858-1).

- *Your Spiritual Gifts Inventory,* by Charles V. Bryant (Nashville: Upper Room Books, 1997. ISBN 0-8358-0819-X).

The Stewardship of One's Money and Possessions

- *Giving and the Gospel.* (Nashville: General Board of Discipleship, 1999.) Video available from the Center for Christian Stewardship, General Board of Discipleship.
- *Holy Smoke! Whatever Happened to Tithing?* by J. Clif Christopher and Herb Mather (Nashville: Discipleship Resources, 1999. ISBN 0-88177-284-4).
- *A Woman's Book of Money and Spiritual Vision* by Rosemary C. Williams (Philadelphia: Innisfree Press, Inc., 2001. ISBN 1880913445).

Financial Stewardship in the Church

- *Abingdon Guide to Funding Ministry,* by Donald W. Joiner and Norma Wimberly (Nashville: Abingdon Press, 1996. ISBN 0-687-01989-3).
- *Achieving Dreams Beyond the Budget: How to Increase Giving in Your Church* (Nashville: General Board of Discipleship, 1999). Available from the Center for Christian Stewardship, General Board of Discipleship.
- *Creating a Climate for Giving,* by Donald W. Joiner (Nashville: Discipleship Resources, 2001. ISBN 0-88177-318-2).
- *Don't Shoot the Horse ('Til You Know How to Drive the Tractor): Moving From Annual Fund Raising to a Life of Giving,* by Herb Mather (Nashville: Discipleship Resources, 1994. ISBN 0-88177-136-8).
- *Faith and Money: Understanding Annual Giving in the Church,* by Michael Reeves and Jennifer Tyler (Nashville: Discipleship Resources, 2003. ISBN 0-88177-410-3).
- *Guidelines for Leading Your Congregation: Finance,* by Wayne C. Barrett and Donald W. Joiner (Nashville: Cokesbury, 2004. ISBN 0-687-03570-8).
- *Giving*. (Ecumenical Center for Stewardship Studies, 1100 West 42nd Street, Suite 225, Indianapolis, IN 46208). An annual publication for clergy and other church leaders.
- *Sharing God's Gifts.* (free from United Methodist Communications).
- *Plain Talk About Churches and Money,* by Dean Hoge, Patrick McNamara, and Charles Zech (Bethesda, Md.: Alban Institute, 1998. ISBN 1-56699-185-4).
- *Revolutionizing Christian Stewardship for the 21st Century,* by Dan R. Dick (Nashville: Discipleship Resources, 1998. ISBN 0-88177-212-7).